M000073148

DULCIMER
CHORD
BOOK

▼ ▼ ▼ ▼ ▼ ▼

**Contributing Authors: Janita Baker, Ron Ewing,
Rick Scott, Michael Rugg, Holly Tannen,
Robert Force & Albert d'Ossché
Music Theory Advisors:
Harriet Jacoff & Bob Burnett
Editors: Elizabeth Bozzi & Craig W. Johnson
Typesetting: Stevie Abrams (The Typesetters)**

Design: Longenecker/Piquett Graphics Studio

▼ ▼ ▼ ▼ ▼ ▼

by Neal Hellman

1 2 3 4 5 6 7 8 9 0

▼ ▼ ▼ ▼ ▼ ▼

TABLE OF CONTENTS

Using the Chart 5
The Multi-Modal Method 7
Using A Capo *by Ron Ewing* 12
What Is A Mode? 13
What Key Is It In? 16
Double Dulcimer *by Robert Force & Albert d'Ossché* . . 18
Tuning To The Modes 20
Some Popular Modes 21

The Chords

Mixolydian Mode 22
Ionian Mode 27
Dorian Mode 33
"Jazz" Tuning 39
Aeolian Mode 44
Lydian Mode 50
Four String Chromatic Tuning *by Janita Baker* 54
Chords for Four Separate Strings 55
Playing Dulcimer In Jam Sessions *by Holly Tannen* . . . 57

Appendices

Fretboard Diagram of Each Mode In The Book 59
History of the Modes 60

UTILIZING THE DULCIMER CHORD CHART WITH SUCCESS FOR ANY TUNING

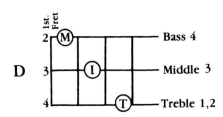

Written above is a sample from the chart. The line on the bottom represents the treble or first pair of strings. The line down the center is the middle string and the line on the top is the bass string. T, I, M and R represent the fingers:

    T   =   Thumb
    I   =   Index finger
    M   =   Middle finger
    R   =   Ring finger

These are, of course, suggested fingerings. Find what works best for you. The letter on top of the chord box (D in this example) is the chord being played. The lowest fret is shown on the right of the top line.

In this example the thumb, index and middle fingers are pressing down to the left of the 4th. fret (treble strings), 3rd. fret (middle string) and 2nd. fret of the bass string respectively. We are playing a D Major chord.

There is an abundance of useful chords for all 7 modes: Mixolydian, Ionian, Aeolian, Dorian, Locrian, Phrygian, Lydian and a "Jazz" tuning.

All the information on the following charts is written out for the Standard Modes. If you do not use the standard tunings or if you tune to different keys, don't despair. Read on and find out how these charts can facilitate almost any tuning and every key.

Let us start by defining an important term, the keytone. The keytone is the "do", or home note, of the key you are tuning into. D is the keytone for the key of D, G for the key of G, and so on. Therefore, a Standard Mode can be defined as a mode in which the keytone is always on the bass string. The middle string is the 5th. note of the scale, or the "sol" note.

For example, in the Standard Mixolydian Mode of D (DD-A-D), the D on the bass is our keytone, the middle string is a 5th. above the keytone (see tuning instructions) and the treble strings are an octave above the bass. In the Standard Aeolian Mode of D (CC-A-D), once again D is the keytone, the middle string is a 5th. above and the treble strings are a 7th. above the bass. All the modes on the charts are Standard Modes.

Now what if you do not tune to the Standard Modes? Chances are you might be using what I like to call the New Mode. In the New Mode, the keytone is on the middle string and the bass note is the 5th., or "sol" note, on the scale. DD-D-A is the New Mixolydian of D and CC-D-A is the New Aeolian of D.

To utilize the chart for a New Mode, reverse the middle and bass strings. A 4/3/2 chord would become 4/2/3 or a 7/6/5 would become 7/5/6, etc. From my experience as a teacher and player, here are some popular New Modes folks are using:

New Mixolydian of A:	AA-A-E
New Dorian of G:	CC-G-D
New Aeolian of A:	GG-A-E
New Ionian of G:	DD-G-D
New Aeolian of B:	AA-B-F#
New Locrian of G:	EbEb-G-D

Once again the New Modes all have the keytone on the middle string and the bass is the 5th. note of the keytone.

If the chart gives the chords for the Mixolydian of D and you are tuned to the Standard Mixolydian of A (AA-E-A) or the Standard Dorian of E (AA-B-E), and the chart is for the Dorian of D (GG-A-D), one must learn the simple art of **transposition.**

TRANSPOSITION

A pitchpipe (circular), piano or any other source of known pitch will prove to be of great help. So will the Wheel of Transposition. The letter names on the wheel correspond to the notes of a pitchpipe or piano keyboard.

Wheel of Transposition

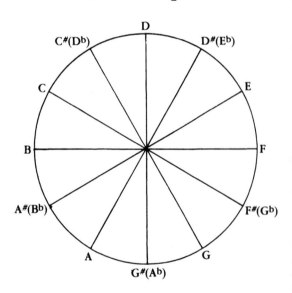

There are 12 different tones in the western musical compass (some of which have more than one name, to make writing easier). When you have moved through all 12, you are back where you started, only an octave higher or lower. It's called an octave because most scales and modes contain 7 different notes, the 8th. being a repeat of the 1st.

Now suppose you wish to play in the Mixolydian of A (AA-E-A) rather than the Mixolydian of D, which is on the charts. Let's look at the wheel. It takes 5 spaces going counterclockwise, from D to A. So if you wish to transpose a chord from the key of D to the key of A, just count 5 spaces counterclockwise from the given note in the D tuning to its counterpart in the A tuning. Thus, D will become an A chord, G will become a D chord, A will become an E chord, etc.

The principle is the same when tuning to a piano. Count the number of piano keys between D, your reference point, and the key to which you are tuning.

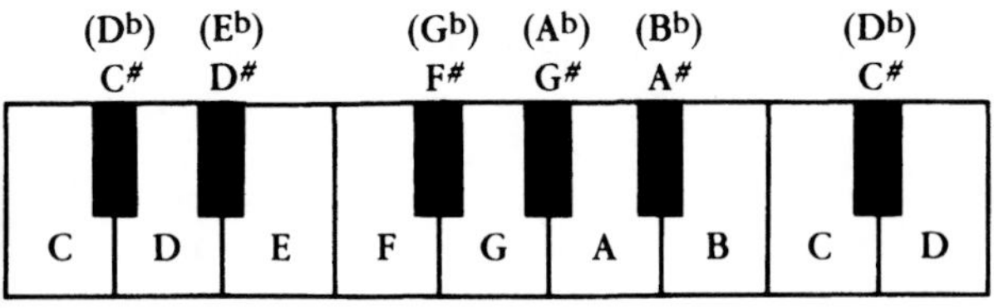

(D♭)	(E♭)		(G♭)	(A♭)	(B♭)		(D♭)	
C♯	D♯		F♯	G♯	A♯		C♯	
C	D	E	F	G	A	B	C	D

Thus, there are five piano keys between D and A (going from right to left). So a G in the key of D is a D in the key of A.

Say, once again, you are transposing from the key of D to the key of A, this time to find what an E chord (in the key of D) would be in the key of A. Using the wheel, count clockwise, because it's the shortest and easiest route. There are 2 spaces between D and E. Now count 2 spaces from A and we arrive at B. Therefore, an E chord in the key of D would be a B chord in the key of A.

A Quick Review

STEP #1: Find out if you are in the Standard Mode or New Mode.

STEP #2: Make the conversion to the Standard Mode from the New Mode. That is, reverse the middle and bass string values of all the chords on the given chart.

STEP #3: Transpose to your own desired key.

Important Note: There are other methods and techniques of playing the dulcimer. "Over the top" is standing while holding the dulcimer from a strap or guitar style. Explore which fingerings work best for you. Fingerings given on the chart are for the lap method. In other words, someone playing over the top, guitar style, will use barred chords instead of the thumb, which is frequently used in the lap method.

APPALACHIAN DULCIMER: THE MULTI-MODAL METHOD

Evolution of technique and style on an instrument is inevitable. Within the last thirty years all of the major acoustic instruments have gone through incredible changes. Musicians like Bill Monroe, Frank Wakefield and David Grisman have radically altered the concepts of playing the mandolin. Earl Scruggs and Tony Trischka have done the same for the five string banjo. There has also been an increased awareness in playing style of the fiddle, guitar and hammered dulcimer.

The same is true for the Appalachian or plucked dulcimer. Jean Ritchie and Richard Fariña brought the dulcimer out of the mountains to the ears of people in urban areas. Since the death of Fariña, an abundance of new dulcimer players have come onto the acoustic music "scene". Due to the dulcimer renaissance of the late 60's to the present, the instrument is taking on a new presence in the music world.

Each area of North America has its own indigenous style of playing. Folks up in British Columbia play the dulcimer from underneath (guitar style) due to the popularity of Rick Scott and the Pied Pear. Robert Force and Albert d'Ossché have popularized the stand up "over the top" technique in the West. Howie Mitchell, Kevin Roth and Lorraine Lee have been a large influence in the Northeast. California has its own methods, too. Michael Rugg, Ken Stedman and Peter Tummerup have influenced the playing styles of many people.

A technique that can enhance good style and help your overall playing is what I like to call the Multi-Modal Method. This method can help ease one of the great problems of dulcimer players—constant retuning. The notion or attitude that the dulcimer can be played only in the mode and key it is tuned to is wrong. This notion has kept the dulcimer from receiving the respect it deserves as a valid musical instrument.

The basic principles of the Multi-Modal Method are:
1) When tuned to the Mixolydian Mode of D (DD-A-D) one can play both melody lines and back-up chords of:
   a) Mixolydian Mode of D (Key of D Major)
   b) Ionian Mode of G (Key of G Major)
   c) Aeolian Mode of B (Bm)
   d) Ionian Mode of D (D Major)
   e) Dorian Mode of A (Am)
   f) Aeolian Mode of E (Em)
2) By using bar chords, melody notes can also be played for:
   a) Dorian Mode of E (Em)
   b) Phrygian Mode of B (Bm)
   c) Dorian Mode of A (Am)
   d) Ionian Mode of G (G Major)

All these modes and keys are possible in the Mixolydian Mode of D (DD-A-D).

Let us start with D Major. The Mixolydian Mode is simply played from the open first strings to the 7th fret. The same scale can also be played using the following chords.

Mixolydian of D

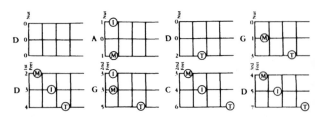

The line on the bottom represents the first two strings, the middle line is the middle string and the line on the top is the bass string.

Try at first playing simple tunes you already know with these chords, like "London Bridge" and "Bile 'em Cabbage Down". The melody is still on the first strings but your dulcimer now takes on a more chordal and less drone disposition. If you are having trouble, just practice the scale and finger positions.

With these chords the dulcimer can be used as back-up instrument. When done correctly the dulcimer can fabricate a wall of sound through which a lead instrument or voice can weave a melody.

The Ionian Mode of D is played on the middle string from the 3rd. fret to the 10th. Here are some simple parallel chords to illustrate the Ionian Mode of D.

Ionian of D

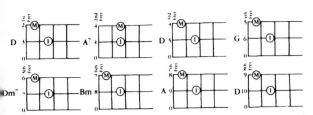

Once again try simple tunes at first, like "Three Blind Mice" and "Jesse James", utilizing just the middle string. Then add the chords by playing harmony notes on the bass string.

An Ionian Mode of D can also be played by utilizing the bass and middle string, starting with the open bass string to the 3rd. fret, then to the open middle string up to the 3rd. fret.

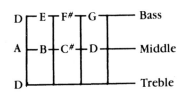

This scale is especially good for flat picking. Using a firm pick, try playing "Arkansas Traveler" and "The 8th of January".

All three techniques can be combined for any song or tune in the key of D. You can play the melody of "Arkansas Traveler" on the middle string, then switch to the bass and middle string scale. When another instrument is taking a break, back it up with the Mixolydian chords. Experiment. Don't be afraid to try something new.

A quick review. So far in the Mixolydian we have:
1) Mixolydian melody on the first strings.
2) Mixolydian chords with the melody still on the first string.
3) Ionian scale on the middle string.
4) Ionian chords with melody still on the middle string.
5) Ionian scale on the bass and middle strings.

We will refer to the key of D Major (Mixolydian and Ionian) as the Open Position.

Using the following finger positions you can play in the Aeolian Mode of E (Em). This technique is called the First Position.

Aeolian of E (Em)

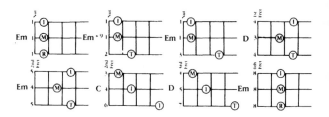

These positions are by no means finite. You could use 6/6/6 for a C chord or 4/3/2 for a D chord. It all depends on what sound you wish to produce. A 4/3/2 sounds more major than a 4/3/4. Let the tone coloring of the tune be your guide to choice of chords. Now try simple tunes that you can already play in this mode, "Shady Grove" and "Rain and Snow". If you have the extra fret (6½), a Dorian Mode of E would be possible.

If you do not have the 6½ fret, you can still play the Dorian Mode of E (key of Em). There is a Dorian scale starting with the 1st. fret of the bass string to the 4th. fret. The A note can be played on the bass or the middle string, so it's up to you.

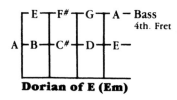

Dorian of E (Em)

You don't have to bar the 1st. fret all the time. When an Em tune goes to a D chord you can, of course, play the dulcimer in the Open Position until you return to the root chord (Em). Try "The Road to Lisdoonvarna" or "Shady Grove". As with the Open Position, the Aeolian chords can be used to back-up other instruments.

Starting in the third position 3/3/3, you can play both melody and chords for the Ionian Mode of G (G Major). These three finger chords might hurt your hand a little, but stay with it and practice the scale.

Ionian Mode of G

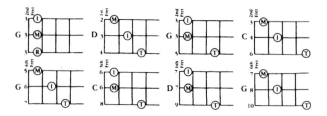

Start with good old "Bile 'em Cabbage Down," "Waterbound" and "Buffalo Gals". The melody is still on the first string, so just sound it out on the melody and then add the chords.

As with the previous position, you can play an Ionian of G flatpick style. Bar the 3rd. fret and play the following scale with your thumb, from the 3rd. fret of the bass string to the 6th., then the 3rd. fret of the middle string to the 6th.

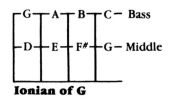

Ionian of G

I use this Third Position often because I love the crisp and melodic sound it produces. When you find you are adapting well to the scale try some more involved tunes like "Old Mother Flannagan" and "Planxty Fanny Powers".

The Fourth Position (4/4/4) will produce a Dorian Mode of A (Am). The Scale goes from 4/4/4 to 11/0/11.

Dorian of A (Am)

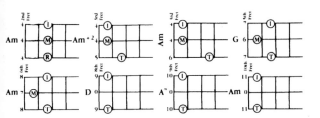

Try "Pretty Polly", "Matty Groves" or "The Blacksmith". The Youngbloods sang a simple tune in the Dorian Mode called "Darkness Darkness", which some of you older dulcimer players might remember.

As with the previous positions there is an easy way to flatpick the melody in the Dorian Mode, from the 4th. fret of the bass to the 7th. fret, then the 4th. fret of the middle to the 7th.

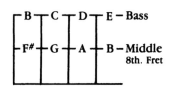

Don't forget you can use the Dorian chords to backup a melody line or your voice. If you are singing with your dulcimer try just playing the melody as an introduction, then use the chords behind your voice.

A Phrygian Mode of B (Bm) can be played by barring the 5th. fret. Starting with the 5th. fret of the bass string go to the 8th. fret, then from the 5th. fret of the middle string to the 8th. fret.

```
┌─B─┬─C─┬─D─┬─E─ Bass
│   │   │   │
├─F#─┼─G─┼─A─┼─B─ Middle
│   │   │   │      8th. Fret
│   │   │   │
└   │   │   │
```

A much more versatile and accessible key of Bm is possible in this tuning. Starting with 0/1/2 we have an Aeolian Mode of B (Bm).

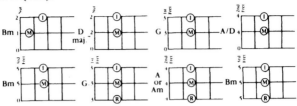

Using a Capo In the DD-A-D Tuning
Ron Ewing & Neal J. Hellman

Another method to put many modes and keys "instantly" at your fingertips is to use a capo. A very workable capo can be obtained from Ron Ewing (please see below).

Scales can be played across the fingerboard as well as on each individual string. 1 = the first string or first pair, 2 = the middle string, 3 = the bass string. When the 6½ fret is utilized it will be noted. Otherwise, please use the 6th fret. Obviously, when you use the 6½ fret you don't use the 6th and vice versa. When we have a scale that starts on the 1st or 3rd string and goes onto the middle string it will be noted by [ ].

Place Capo at:

1st Fret (EE-B-E)
Aeolian of E (Em).	Strings 1 & 3 Frets 1-8
Dorian of E (Em)	Strings 1 & 3 Frets 1-8 (6½)
Dorian of E (Em)	[Strings 1 *or* 3 Frets 1-4 (E, F♯, G, A) [String 2 Frets 1-4 (B, C♯, D, E)]
Dorian of E (Em)	String 2 Frets 4-11
Mixolydian of E	String 2 Frets 4-11 (6½)

2nd Fret (F♯F♯-C♯-F♯)
Locrian of F♯ (F♯m)	Strings 1 & 3 Frets 2-9
Locrian of C♯ (C♯m)	String 2 Frets 2-9
Phrygian of F♯ (F♯m)	Strings 1 & 3 Frets 2-9 (6½)
Phrygian of C♯ (C♯m)	String 2 Frets 2-9 (6½)

3rd Fret (GG-D-G)
Ionian of G	Strings 1 & 3 Frets 3-10
Ionian of G	[Strings 1 *or* 3 Frets 3-6 (G, A, B, C) [String 2 Frets 3-6 (D, E, F♯, G)]

4th Fret (AA-E-A)
Dorian of A (Am)	Strings 1 & 3 Frets 4-11
Dorian of A (Am)	[Strings 1 *or* 3 Frets 4-7 (A, B, C, D) [String 2 Frets 4-7 (E, F♯, G, A)]
Mixolydian of A	Strings 1 & 3 Frets 4-11 (6½)
Mixolydian of A	[Strings 1 *or* 3 Frets 4-7 (6½) (A, B, C♯, D) [String 2 Frets 4-7 (E, F♯, G, A)]
Ionian of A	[Strings 1 *or* 3 Frets 4-7 (6½) (A, B, C♯, D) [String 2 Frets 4-7 (6½) (E, F♯, G♯, A)]

5th Fret (BB-F♯-B)
Aeolian of B (Bm)	Strings 1 & 3 Frets 5-12 (6½)
Aeolian of B (Bm)	[Strings 1 *or* 3 Frets 5-8 (6½) (B, C♯, D, E) [String 2 Frets 5-8 (F♯, G, A, B)]
Dorian of B (Bm)	[Strings 1 *or* 3 Frets 5-8 (6½) (B, C♯, D, E) [String 2 Frets 5-8 (6½) (F♯, G♯, A, B)]
Phrygian of B (Bm)	Strings 1 & 3 Frets 5-12

6th Fret (CC-G-C)
Lydian of C	String 1 & 3 Frets 6-13

For information on dulcimer capos, please write:
Ron Ewing
234 East Duncam
Columbus, Ohio 43202
(614) 263-7246

WHAT IS A MODE?

A mode is a sequence of tones and semi-tones within a musical scale.

What differentiates one mode from another is the various combinations of tones and semi-tones.

Until the sixteenth century the seven modes dominated all written western music. Unlike today's chromatic scale of 12 notes, modes contained only eight, with the last note an octave of the first. They are called diatonic modes due to the arrangement of the tones and semi-tones—four whole and two ½ tones. We will examine the various combinations of the seven modes by using a number of reference points.

To begin, let us examine all the ½ tones that exist in our chromatic scale. This is our first reference point.

½	½	½	½	½	½	½	½	½	½	½	½
D	D#	E	F	F#	G	G#	A	A#	B	C	C#	D
	(Eb)			(Gb)		(Ab)		(Bb)			(Db)	

Note how the scale is divided into ½ tones. Going from E to F is ½ step while G to A is a whole step. Two ½ steps = 1 whole step.

Our second reference point will be the dulcimer fingerboard when tuned to the Mixolydian of D (DD-A-D). This is done to correspond with the "Multi-Modal Method" technique.

D (open)

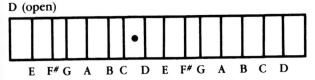

E F#G A B C D E F#G A B C D

Our third reference point will be the key of C. Viewing all the modes in the same key gives a clear understanding of a "flatted" third or a "sharpened" fourth.

The Ionian Mode of C: C, D, E, F, G, A, B, C is the same as our modern major scale. The Ionian Mode starts on the 3rd. fret and ends with the octave on the 10th. Using our first reference point (chromatic scale) let's count the steps and ½ steps within this mode:

1st. Note	2nd. Note	3rd. Note	4th. Note	5th. Note	6th. Note	7th. Note	Octave 8th. Note
C	D	E	F	G	A	B	C
Step 1	Step 1	Step ½	Step 1	Step 1	Step 1	Step ½	

Therefore the combination for the Ionian Mode is step-step-½ step-step-step-step-½ step. No other other mode will have this exact combination of steps and ½ steps.

Even though the Ionian mode is for the key of G in our Multi-Modal Method, the steps and ½ steps will be the same.

G	A	B	C	D	E	F	G
		½				½	
step	step	step	step	step	step	step	

13

Review: A mode is a sequence of tones and semitones within a musical scale. Each mode has its own combination of tones and semitones (steps and ½ steps).

The steps and ½ steps within a particular mode will always be the same, regardless of the key.

The Mixolydian Mode of C: C, D, E, F, G, A, Bb, C. It is similar to the Ionian Mode but has a flatted 7th., a Bb instead of a B. If you look on the chromatic reference chart you can easily see that Bb is ½ under or flatter than B. Here are the steps and ½ step combinations for the Mixolydian Mode.

1st. Note	2nd. Note	3rd. Note	4th. Note	5th. Note	6th. Note	7th. Note	Octave 8th. Note
C	D	E	F	G	A	Bb	C
step	step	½ step	step	step	½ step	step	

Once again we have the same combination for the key of D (the key used in the Multi-Modal Method).

D	E	F#	G	A	B	C	D
1	1	½	1	1	½	1	

The Aeolian Mode (1st. fret - 8th. fret) in the key of C is: C, D, Eb, F, G, Ab, Bb, C. Note this mode has a flatted 3rd., 6th. and 7th. note. The flatted 3rd. is why this is called a minor mode.

1st. Note	2nd. Note	3rd. Note	4th. Note	5th. Note	6th. Note	7th. Note	Octave 8th. Note
C	D	Eb	F	G	Ab	Bb	C
step	½ step	step	step	½ step	step	step	

Multi-Modal Method Key of Em

E	F#	G	A	B	C	D	E
1	½	1	1	½	1	1	

The Dorian Mode (4th. fret - 11th. fret) in the key of C is: C, D, Eb, F, G, A, Bb, C. Note once again a flatted 3rd., making it a minor mode. This is similar to the Aeolian but does not have a flatted 6th.

1st. Note	2nd. Note	3rd. Note	4th. Note	5th. Note	6th. Note	7th. Note	Octave 8th. Note
C	D	Eb	F	G	A	Bb	C
step	½ step	step	step	step	½ step	step	

Multi-Modal Method Key of Am.

A	B	C	D	E	F#	G	A
1	½	1	1	1	½	1	

Lydian Mode: (6th. fret to 13th. fret). Same as the Ionian Mode except it has a sharpened 4th.: C, D, E, F#, G, A, B, C. The Lydian mode for the Multi-Modal Method is also in the key of C.

1st. Note	2nd. Note	3rd. Note	4th. Note	5th. Note	6th. Note	7th. Note	Octave 8th. Note
C	D	E	F#	G	A	B	C
			½			½	
step	step	step	step	step	step	step	

Phrygian Mode: (5th. fret to 12th fret). Another minor mode (flatted 3rd.) with a flatted 2nd., 6th. and 7th. In the key of C: C, Db, Eb, F, G, Ab, Bb, C. Note except for the flatted 2nd. it is the same as the Aeolian Mode.

1st. Note	2nd. Note	3rd. Note	4th. Note	5th. Note	6th. Note	7th. Note	Octave 8th. Note
C	Db	Eb	F	G	Ab	Bb	C
½				½			
step	step	step	step	step	step	step	

Multi-Modal Method Key of Bm.

B	C	D	E	F#	G	A	B
½	1	1	1	½	1	1	

Locrian Mode: (2nd. fret to 9th. fret). A very uneven minor scale, in the key of C: C, Db, Eb, F, Gb, Ab, Bb, C.

1st. Note	2nd. Note	3rd. Note	4th. Note	5th. Note	6th. Note	7th. Note	Octave 8th. Note
C	Db	Eb	F	Gb	Ab	Bb	C
½			½				
step	step	step	step	step	step	step	

Multi-Modal Method Key of F#m.

F#	G	A	B	C	D	E	F#
½	1	1	½	1	1	1	

Review: A mode is a sequence of tones and semitones within a musical scale. Each mode has its own combination of tones and semitones (steps and ½ steps).
These steps and ½ steps within a particular mode will always be the same, regardless of the key.

Review of the steps and ½ steps within each mode:

Ionian:	1	1	½	1	1	1	½
Mixolydian:	1	1	½	1	1	½	1
Lydian:	1	1	1	½	1	1	½
Dorian:	1	½	1	1	1	½	1
Aeolian:	1	½	1	1	½	1	1
Phrygian:	½	1	1	1	½	1	1
Locrian:	½	1	1	½	1	1	1

Note: If your dulcimer has the extra (6½) fret it is possible to play the following:

In the Ionian Mode while tuned to the Mixolydian, the 6½ serves as the 7th. note, or B in the key of C.

In the Dorian Mode while tuned to the Aeolian, the 6½ serves as the 6th. note.

In the Phrygian Mode while tuned to the Locrian, the 6½ serves as the 5th. note.

In the Aeolian Mode while tuned to the Phrygian, the 6½ serves as the 2nd. note.

WHAT KEY IS IT IN?
and
WHAT CHORDS DO I PLAY?

So there you are with your dulcimer at the local folk jam. The fiddler starts to play and you lean over to the guitarist and say, "Pardon me, Fred, but what key is this in?" Fred turns around and says "G", and away you go. However, finding the right key is not always that easy. The most common way to find out the key to a song or tune is from sheet music.

Take out any piece of written sheet music that you have. Even if you don't know how to read music you can still tell what key the composition is in by counting the number of sharps and flats on the key signature.

No flats or sharps.
Key of C Major
or its relative
minor: **Am**.

One sharp (F#)
Key of G or Em.

Two sharps
(C# and F#)
Key of D or Bm.

Three sharps
(C#, F# and G#)
Key of A or F#m.

Four sharps
(C#, D#, F# and G#)
Key of E or C#m.

One flat (Bb)
Key of F or Dm.

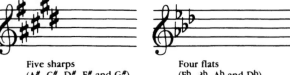

Five sharps
(A#, C#, D#, F# and G#)
Key of B or G#m.

Four flats
(Eb, Bb, Ab and Db)
Key of Ab or Fm.

A tune will usually begin and end with the chord of the key it's in. If the first and last chord is a G, then the tune is in G Major; if the first and last chord is an Em, then the tune is in Em, etc.

Once you know the key, the next step is to find the correct chords. A great deal of folk and traditional music will follow a I, IV, V format, meaning if you're playing in the key of D Major then:

I = **The tonic,** the root chord. D in this example. The chord the tune usually begins and ends on. The first note of the diatonic scale.

IV = **The sub-dominant.** G chord in the key of D. The fourth note of the diatonic scale.

V = **The dominant.** A chord in the key of D. The fifth note in the musical scale.

These chords can be utilized in countless folk songs and tunes. Another frequently used chord is the **Relative Minor,** or the 6th. chord. In the key of D this would be Bm. As a reference guide, the following has been written to aid you in finding the correct chords for most of the major keys.

Table of Major Chord Transpositions

Key	Tonic I•	II	III	Sub Dom. IV•	Dom. V•	Rel. Minor VI•	VII
C	C	Dm	Em	F	G	Am	B dim.
D	D	Em	F#m	G	A	Bm	C# dim.
E	E	F#m	G#m	A	B	C#m	D# dim.
F	F	Gm	Am	Bb	C	Dm	E dim.
G	G	Am	Bm	C	D	Em	F# dim.
A	A	Bm	C#m	D	E	F#m	G# dim.

Once again, for simple back-up playing the most important chords are the tonic (I), sub-dominant (IV), dominant (V) and the relative minor (VI).

When playing chords to back up tunes in the **minor** keys there is a different pattern. Let's use Em as our example. In the key of Em one would probably use the I chord, Em; the VII chord, D, and the III chord, G. Sometimes the IV (in our example, A or Am) chord is used as well. Of course, a multitude of chords might be used depending on the complexity of the composition. Here is a reference guide for the minor keys.

Key	Minor I•	II	III•	IV•	V	VI	VII•
Am	Am	B dim.	C	D or Dm	Em	F	G
Bm	Bm	C# dim.	D	E or Em	F#m	G	A
Cm	Cm	D dim.	Eb	F or Fm	Gm	Ab	Bb
Dm	Dm	E dim.	F	G or Gm	Am	Bb	C
Em	Em	F# dim.	G	A or Am	Bm	C	D
Fm	Fm	G dim.	Ab	Bb or Bbm	Cm	Db	E
Gm	Gm	A dim.	Bb	C or Cm	Dm	Eb	F

As you have read before (Multi-Modal Method), it is possible to play back-up and melody lines in a number of keys and modes within one mode without returning. Please be aware of this.

In the Lydian Mode of C you can play back-up in the keys of G, C, D, Em, Am and Bm. One can play a major key tune while in a Dorian or Aeolian Mode. The potential of the dulcimer as a rhythm instrument is just being explored. Please don't be afraid to experiment with the many chord possibilities in **all** of the modes.

DOUBLE DULCIMER
by R. Force & A. d'Ossché

Over the past ten years we have been continually intrigued and challenged by the possibilities available for two dulcimers played simultaneously in various musical combinations. Not only does the entire harmonic overtone series expand, but the potential for rhythmic and melodic variations is equally enhanced. We have found that there are five basic chordal interactions that occur between us:

1. Playing in exactly parallel positions
2. Chordal inversions where the constituent elements are being melodically juxtaposed
3. Using two different chords (usually a 3rd. or a 5th. apart) to create parallel harmonies
4. Lead lines played over moving chords
5. Moving elements within the chords themselves

The following excerpts are in D-A-D (1-5-1) tuning.

WELLYN

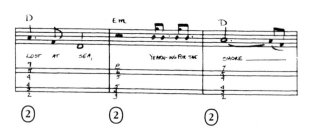

LIKE A SHIP

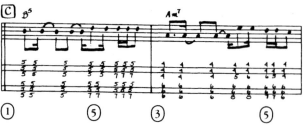

POKERFACE SMILE

FIRENZE

TABAC ALLEGRIA

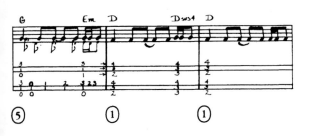

CONVERSATIONS WITH THE RIVER

The complete music, tab and lyrics for these and other songs can be found in *The Wild Dulcimer Songbook*, © R. Force and A. d'Ossché, Kicking Mule Publishing, Inc., P.O. Box 158, Aldernoint, CA 95411. Used by permission.

TUNING TO THE MODES
A QUICK REVIEW

Standard Ionian Mode

— Tune bass to desired keytone.
— Press bass to the left of the 4th. fret and tune all the other strings to this note.
— Example AA-A-D, Ionian of D.

Standard Mixolydian Mode

— Tune bass to keytone.
— Press bass to the left of the 4th. fret and tune the middle string to this note.
— Press bass to the left of the 7th. fret and tune the open 1st. strings to it (DD-A-D).

Standard Dorian Mode

— Tune bass to keytone.
— Press bass to the left of the 4th. fret and tune the middle string to this note.
— Press bass to the left of the 3rd. fret and tune the melody strings to it (GG-A-D).

Standard Aeolian Mode

— Bass to keytone.
— Press bass to the left of the 4th. fret and tune open middle string to this note.
— Press bass to the left of the 6th. fret and tune the melody strings to this note (CC-A-D).

Standard Lydian Mode

— Bass to keytone.
— Press bass to the left of the 4th. fret and tune middle string to this note.
— Press bass to the left of the 1st. fret and tune melody strings to this note (DD-G-C).

Standard Locrian Mode

— Tune the melody strings to a $^b6$ of what you want your keytone to be. Or just tune the melody strings to where it feels good—not too loose or too tight.
— Then press the melody strings to the left of the 2nd. fret and tune the bass string an octave above. Then press the bass string at the 4th. fret and tune the middle string to this note. (AA-G$^\cdot$-C$^\cdot$).

Standard Phrygian Mode

— Bass to keytone.
— Press bass to the left of the 4th. fret and tune **all** the other strings to this note.
— Then press the melody strings at the 2nd. fret and tune it down so that it matches the open 2nd. string (E^bE^b-G-C).

New Modes: Use the middle string as the keytone and proceed as above.

REMEMBER—IN ORDER TO USE THE CHART CORRECTLY YOU MUST CONVERT YOUR NEW MODES TO THE STANDARD ONES. THIS IS DONE BY REVERSING THE MIDDLE AND BASS STANDARDS CHART IF YOU USE A NEW MODE.

VERSING THE MIDDLE AND BASS STRING ON THE
CHART IF YOU USE A NEW MODE.

NOTE: There are tunings that do not conform to our
principles, such as AA-A-A (Mix. of A), DD-A-A (Dorian
of A), GG-E-C (Ionian of C), etc.

SOME POPULAR MODES

	Standard		New	
Ionian	AA-A-D	(key of D)	DD-G-D	(key of G)
	GG-G-C	(key of C)	CC-F-C	(key of F)
	5-5-1		5-1-5	
Mixolydian	DD-A-D	(key of D)	AA-A-E	(key of A)
	1-5-1		1-1-5	
Aeolian	CC-A-D	(Dm)	GG-A-E	(Am)
	BbBb-G-C	(Cm)	AA-B-F#	(Bm)
	7-5-1		7-1-5	
Dorian	GG-A-D	(Dm)	CC-G-D	(Gm)
	AA-B-E	(Em)	DD-A-E	(Am)
	4-5-1		4-1-5	
Lydian	DD-G-C	(C and more)	AA-G-D	(G)
	CC-F-Bb	(Bb)	2-1-5	
	2-5-1			
Phrygian	EbEb-G-C	(Dm)	AbAb-F-C	(Fm)
	b3-5-1		b3-1-5	
Locrian	AA-G#-C#	(C#m)	EbEb-G-D	
	BbBb-A-D	(Dm)	b6-1-5	
	b6-5-1			
Jazz Tunings	DA-A-D	(key of D)		
	DG-A-D	(key of D)		
	DG-G-D	(key of D)		

21

MIXOLYDIAN MODE   DD-A-D (1-5-1)

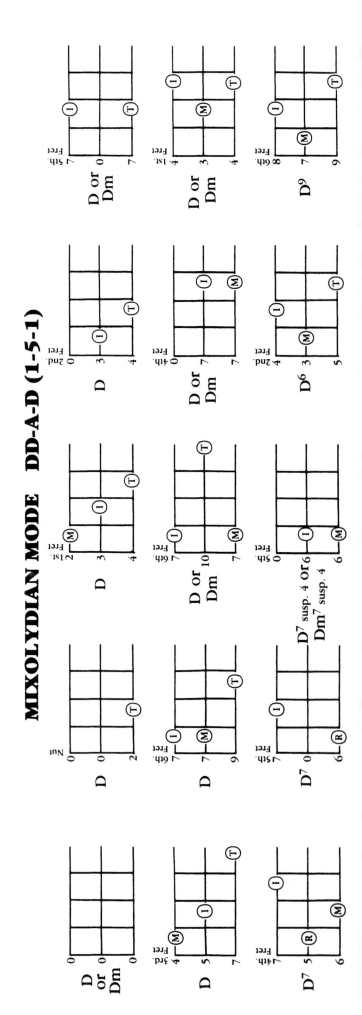

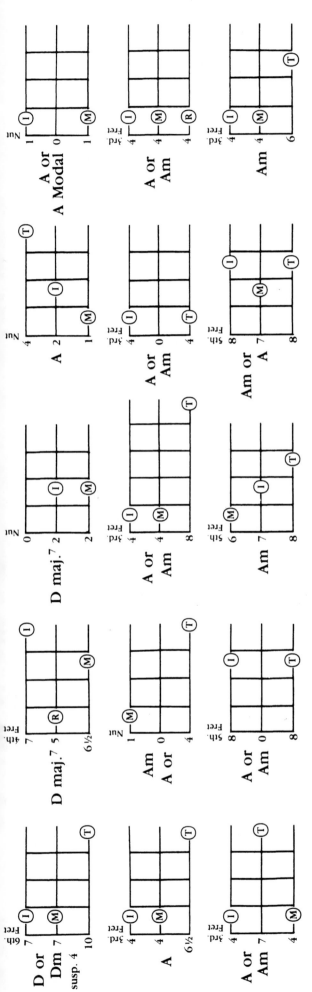

23

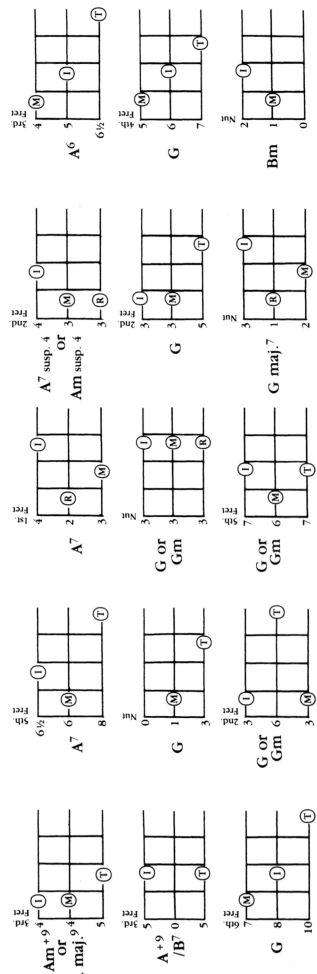

24

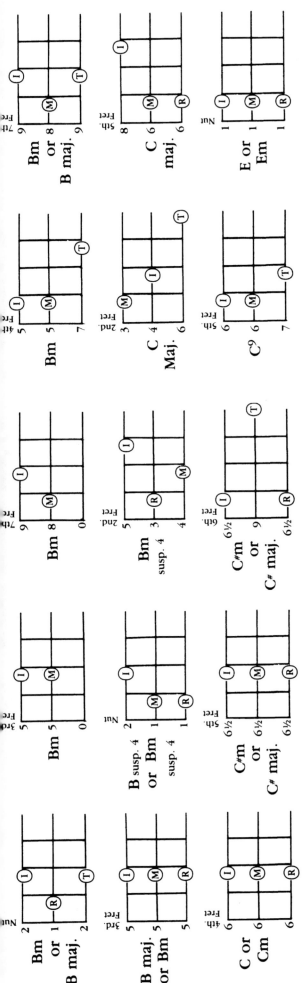

25

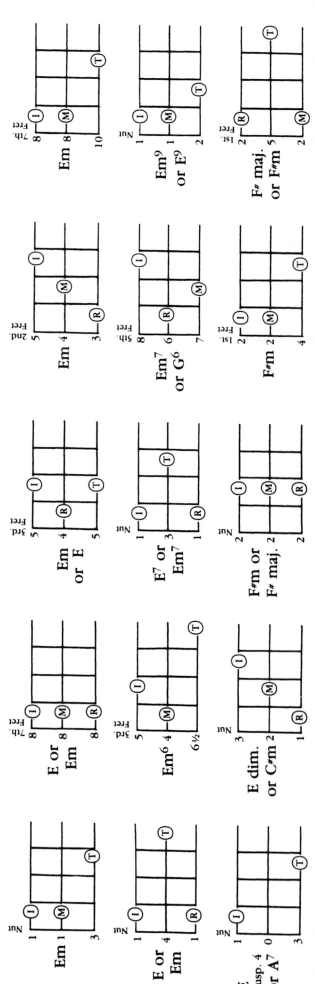

26

IONIAN MODE   AA-A-D (5-5-1)

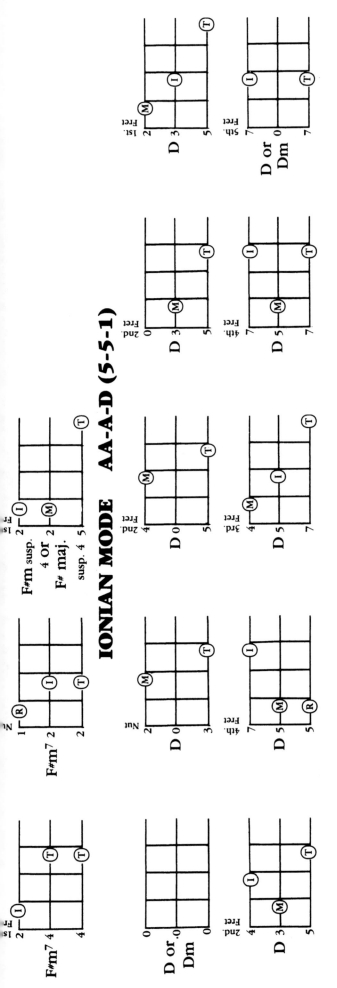

27

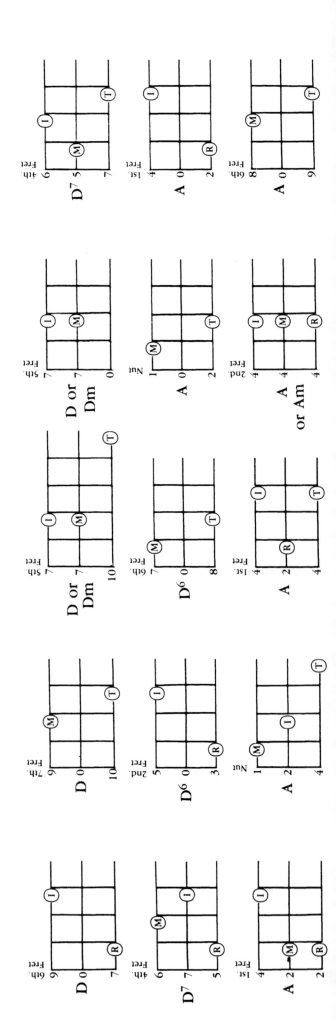

28

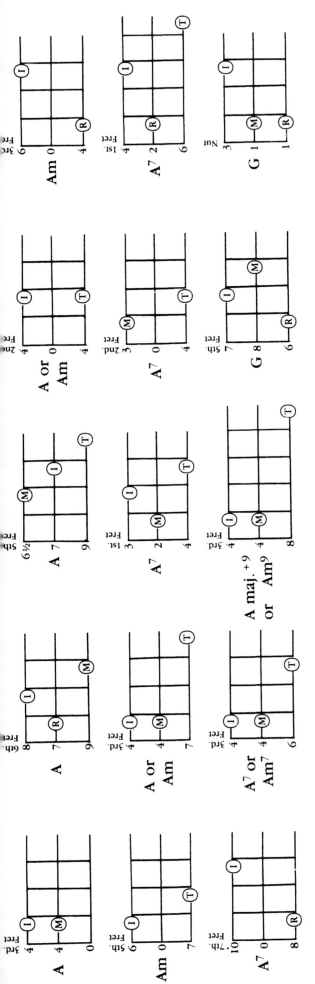

29

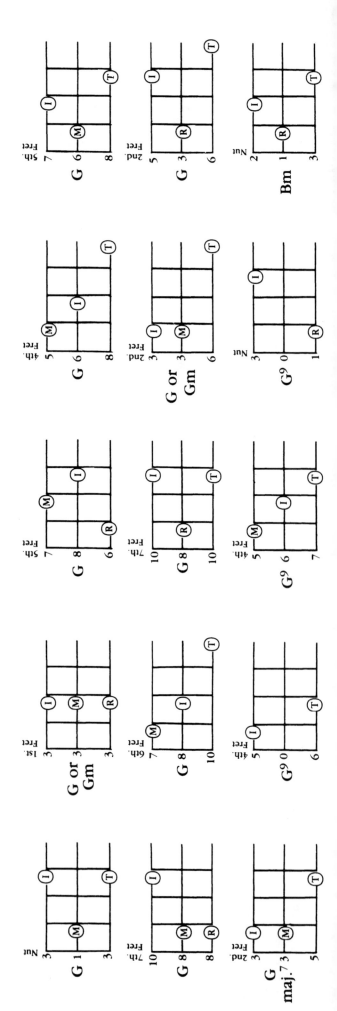

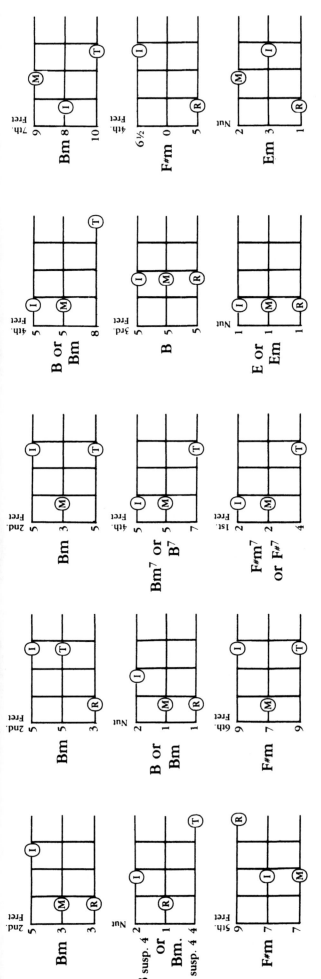

31

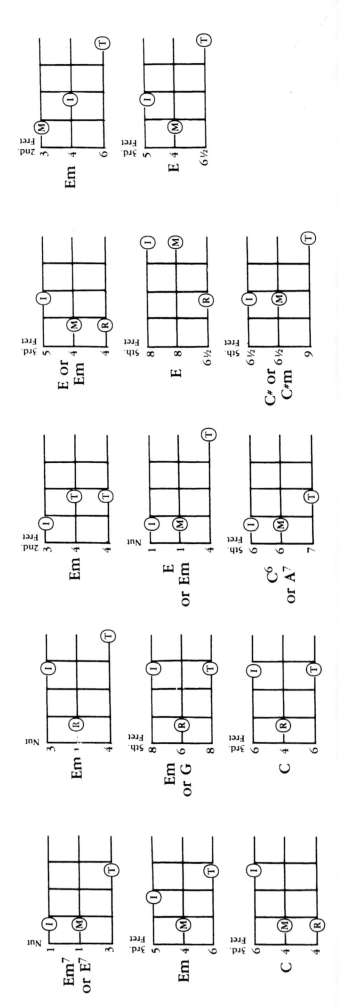

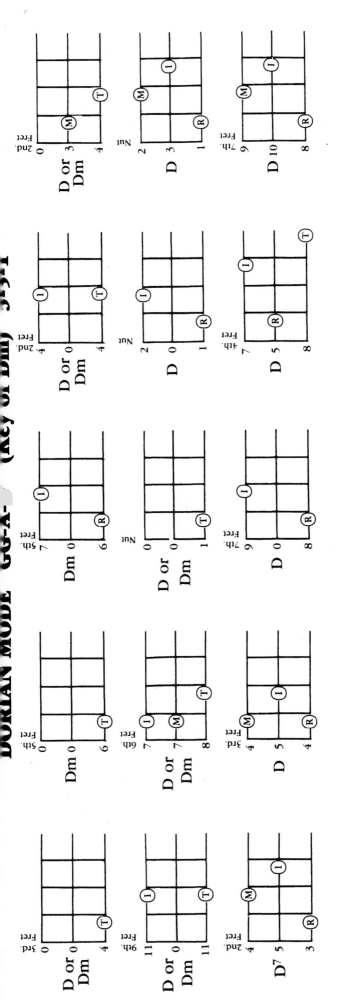

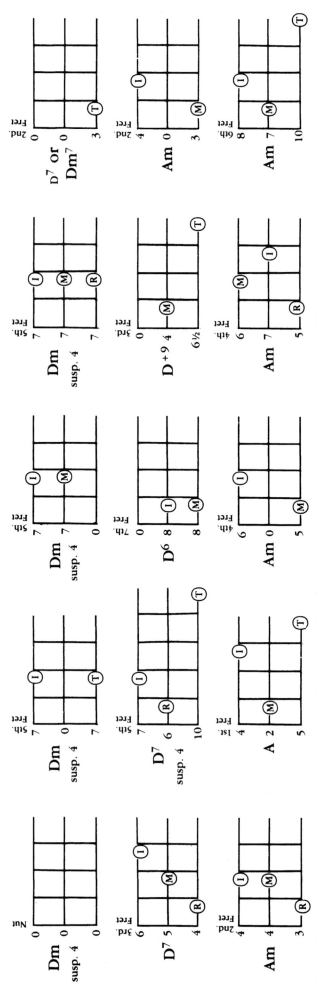

34

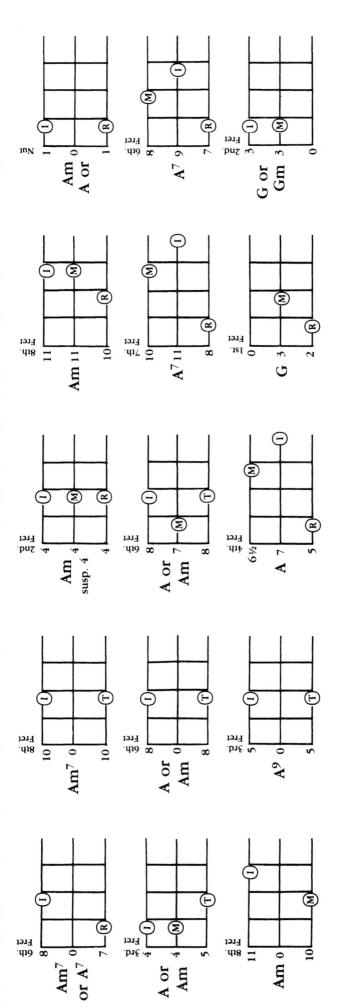

35

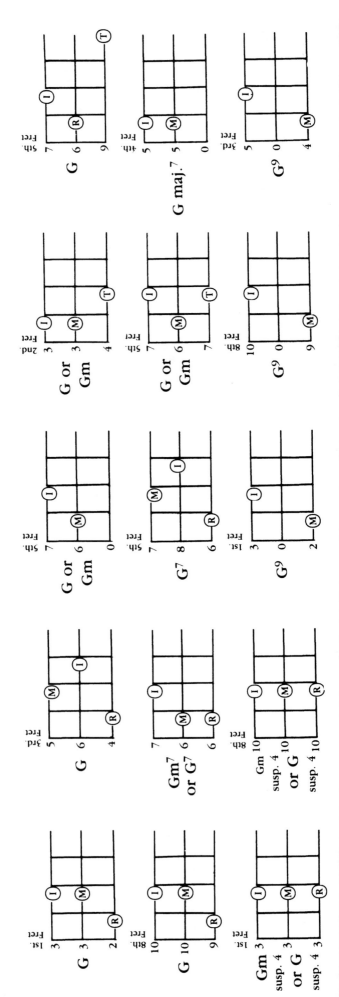

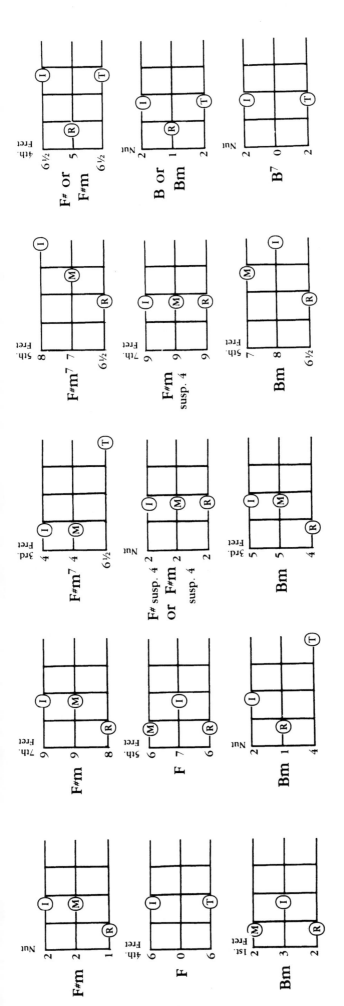

37

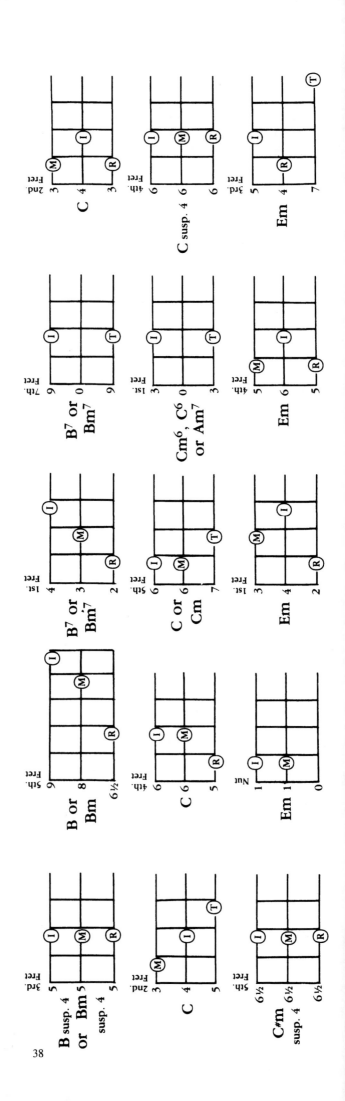

38

JAZZ TUNING DA-A-D 15-5-1

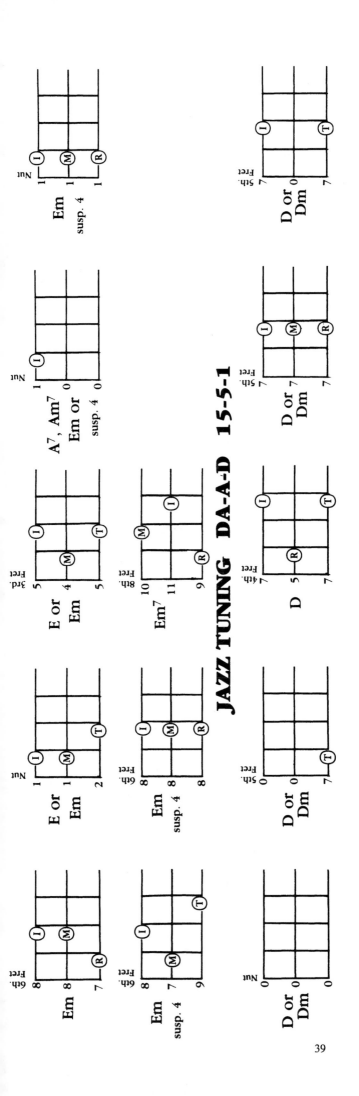

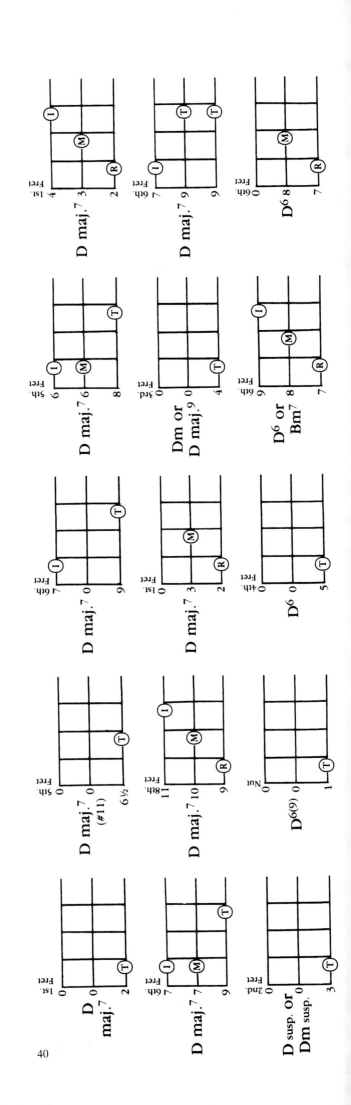

40

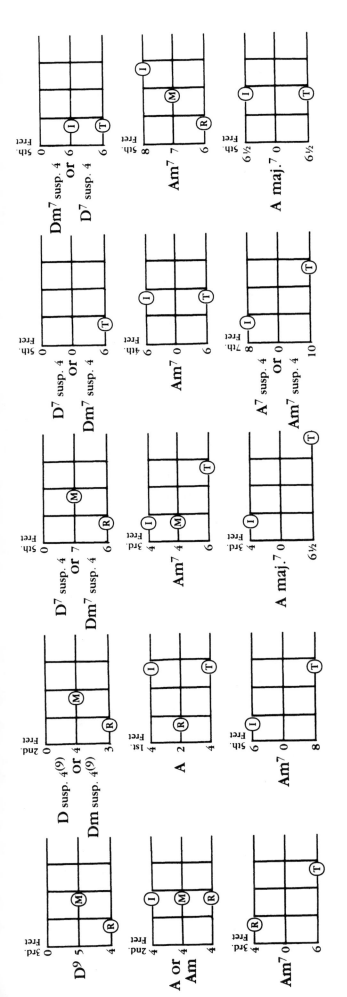

41

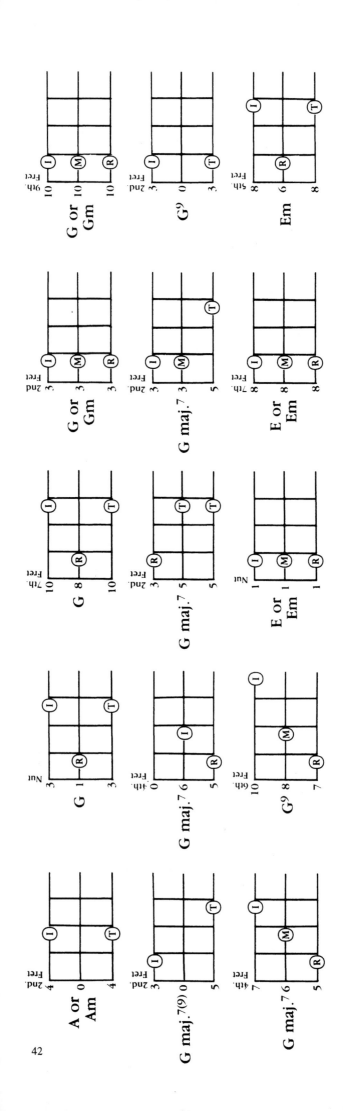

42

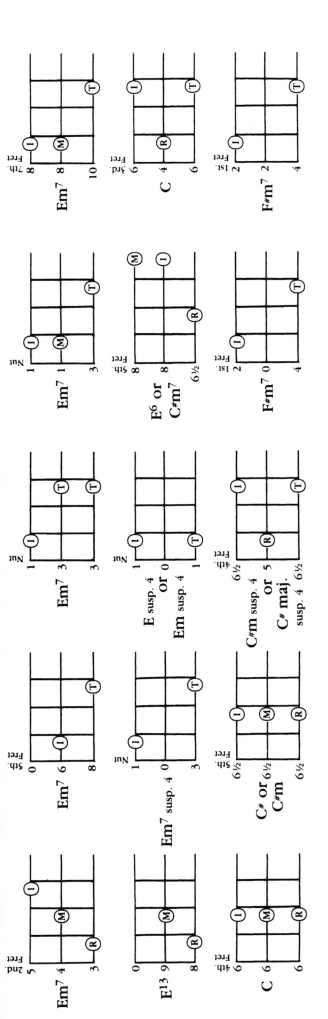

43

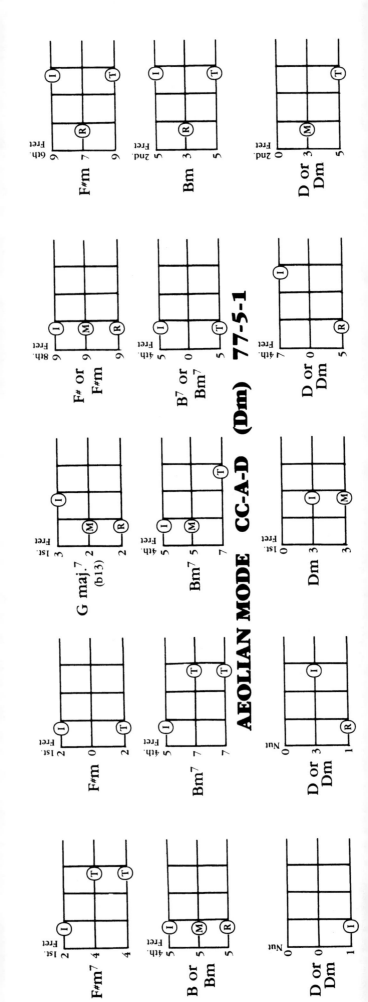

AEOLIAN MODE   CC-A-D   (Dm)   77-5-1

F#m

F# or F#m

G maj.7 (b13)

F#m

F#m7

Bm

B7 or Bm7

Bm7

Bm7

B or Bm

D or Dm

D or Dm

Dm

D or Dm

D or Dm

44

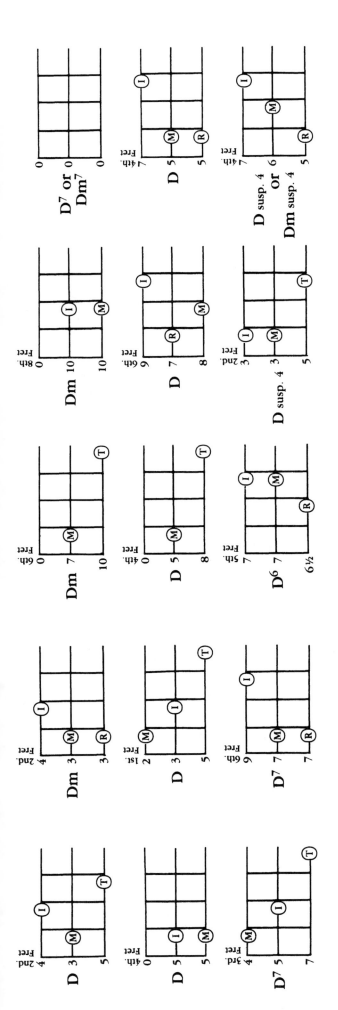

45

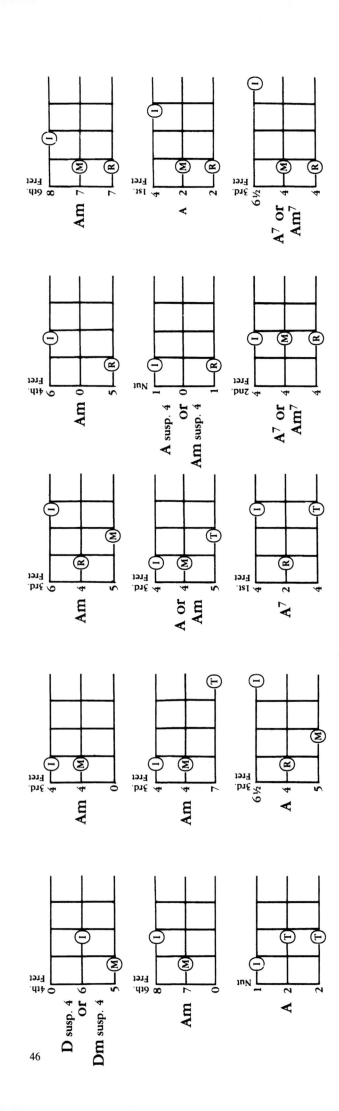

46

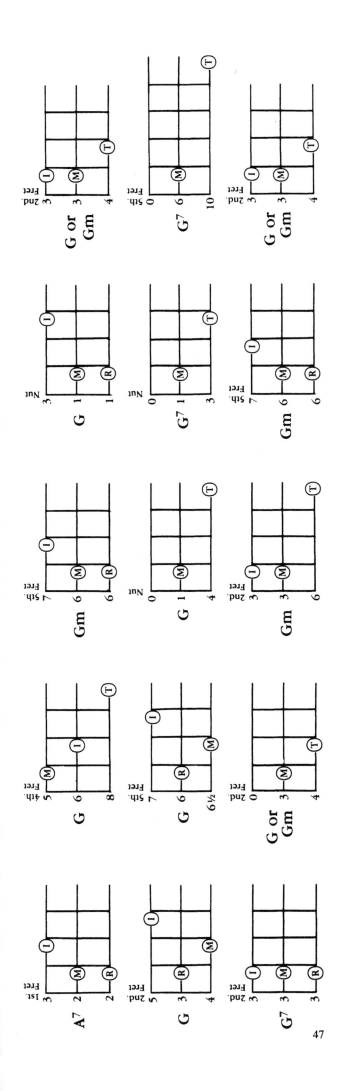

47

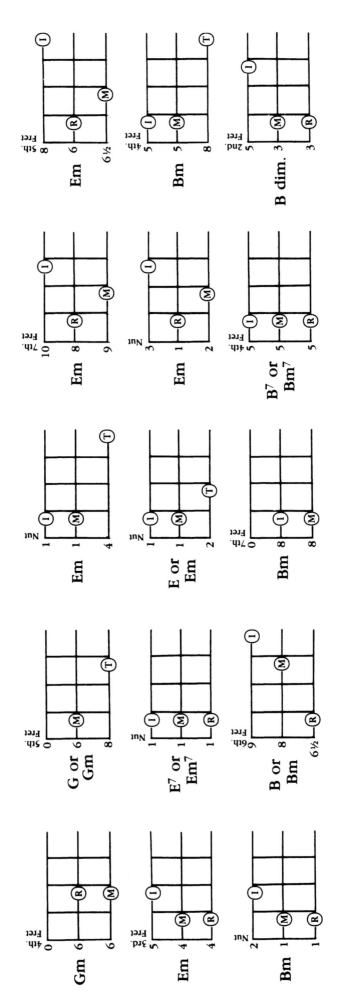

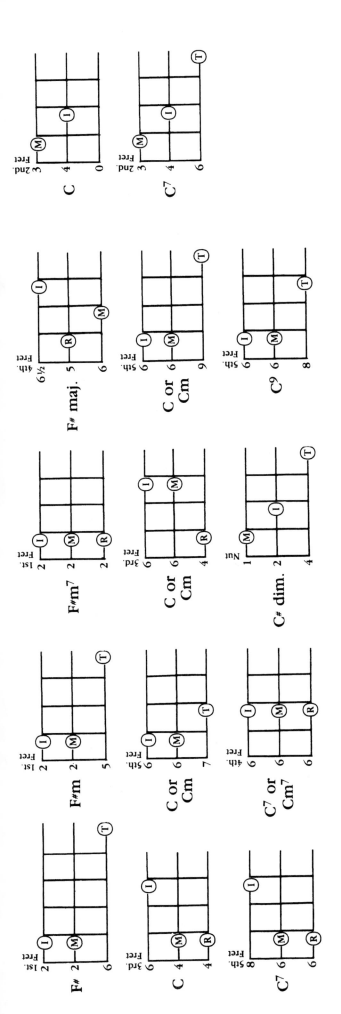

49

LYDIAN MODE DD-G-C 9-5-1

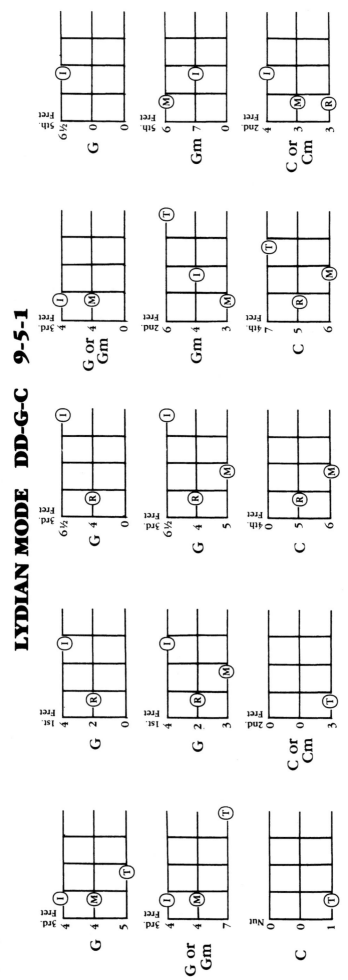

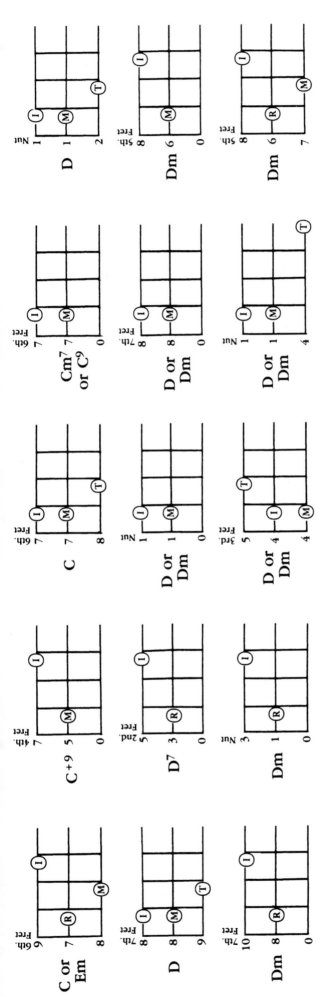

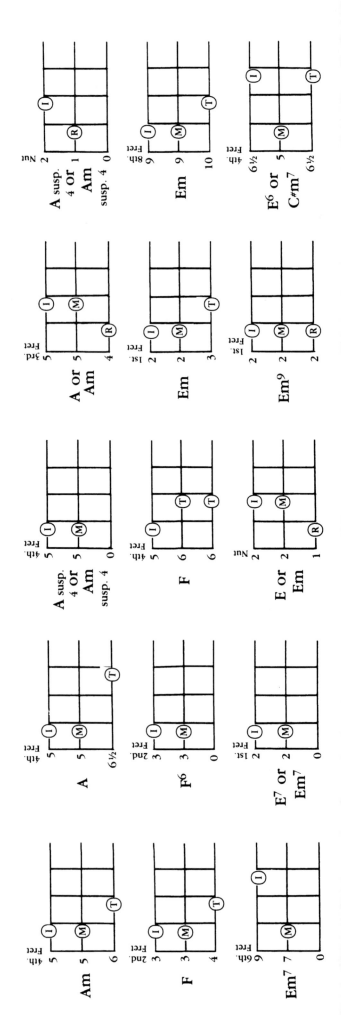

52

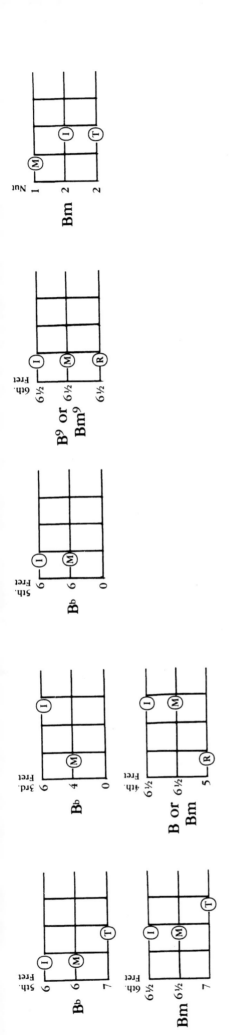

53

FOUR STRING "CHROMATIC" TUNING

Janita Baker

I discovered the delights of four string dulcimer while trying to work out several of Scott Joplin's rags. These required a chromatic (12 note) scale which was unavailable on the dulcimer's standard diatonic fretboard. I found that by evenly spacing the four string and tuning the second string one-half step higher than the middle string when in the Mixolydian mode, I had the complete chromatic scale at hand. By leaving the second string tuned "chromatically" you can tune into any of the other modes and still have the chromatic scale capability.

TUNINGS: Chromatic Mixolydian: DA#AD
Chromatic Ionian: DA#GD or AA#AD
Chromatic Aeolian: CA#AD
etc.

For example in "Chromatic Mixolydian" tuning, you have the following notes:

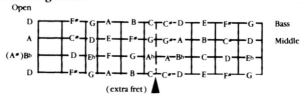

I often find I may note the second string only once or twice in a song, but those few notes are essential to the integrity of the piece. For example, the introduction to "Ragtime Dance" is entirely dependent upon a chromatic scale, while the rest of the song *could* be played without the second string notes (there are only three notes that can't be found elsewhere and you could improvise without them), on the other hand the song loses some of its particular "Joplin-sound" without those notes, and to play them elsewhere on the fingerboard makes it a much more difficult piece to play.

INTRODUCTION TO "RAGTIME DANCE"

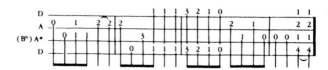

From "Finger Picking Dulcimer", Janita Baker, Measures 1-4, pg 40.
Kicking Mule Publications

Another good use for the four separate string technique is to facilitate playing a piece of music that doesn't necessarily require a chromatic scale, but is simply easier to play, or sounds better with 4 strings. In the following excerpt from F. Sor's "Andante" (second part), the second string is tuned to the middle string (DAAD). You can alternate between the second and third strings, and use the second as an open "drone" to maintain the evenness and sustain of the melody and keep the tune "flowing".

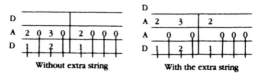

Should you wish to change from finger-picking to strumming, it is easy to drop the second string down into standard tuning (DAAD) and strum in a "normal" three string style. It is not terribly hard to readjust your chording patterns to accommodate the re-arrangement and it can lend a fuller sound to the instrument. It also expands your chording capability: you can usually play a full chord triad and still have an open "drone" string, and in the following examples:

D	0	D	—Bass
A	0	A	—Middle
A	3	D	—Treble
D	2	F#	—Treble

D
Tonic

0	D
1	B
3	D
3	G

G
Dominant

0	D
0	A
3	D
2	F#

A7
Subdom.

Janita Baker's Kicking Mule album (KM 219), "Finger-picking Dulcimer" and accompanying song book are available from:

Janita Baker 4665 Park Hall Road, Santa Margarita, CA 93453
Record: $6.95 Book: $5.95 Shipping: $1.25

CHORDS FOR FOUR EQUIDISTANT STRINGS

Important note: Experiment with the voicing of each chord. Instead of a C major I like to use a C9 or a G sus4. It all depends on the key you're in. Sometimes an Em7 might fit better than an Em. It also depends on the tone color of the composition. Take your time and experiment!

Also, you might have to cut two new notches in the nut and bridge to accomodate the following chords.

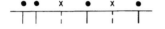

● = existing grooves
x = new grooves
  in nut & bridge

D-D-A-D

Chords	T	T	M	B	Chords	T	T	M	B
D	2-	4-	3-	0	D maj7	2-	0-	2-	4
D	4-	2-	3-	0	D maj7	2-	4-	2-	0
D	4-	2-	0-	4	D maj7	4-	0-	2-	2
D	4-	2-	3-	4	D maj7	4-6½-	5-		0
D	4-	0-	3-	0	D maj7	9-	0-	9-	4
D or Dm	0-	0-	0-	0	D9	1-	2-	3-	0
D	7-	9-	8-	0	D9	4-	1-	0-	2
D	2-	4-	5-	0	D sus4	9-	0-	9-	11
D	7-	9-	7-	0	D sus4	4-	0-	6-	7
D	7-	0-	7-	9	D sus4	10-	8-	8-	8
D	7-	0-	0-	7	D sus4	10-	7-	0-	7
D	7-	0-	5-	4	D min7 (11) or	6-	3-	4-	0
D	7-	4-	5-	0	maj7 (11)				
D	7-	4-	3-	0					
D	7-	0-	7-	7	G	3-	0-	1-	3
D	9-	7-	0-	9	G or Gm	3-	0-	3-	3
D	9-	0-	7-	7	G or Gm	3-	3-	3-	3
D	9-	0-	10-	11	G	3-	5-	3-	0
D or Dm	4-	0-	3-	4	G	3-	0-	3-	5
D or Dm	4-	0-	0-	4	G	3-	0-	6-	5
D	4-	0-	0-	2	G	5-	0-	0-	3
D	9-	11-	10-	0	G	5-	0-	3-	3
D7	6-	2-	3-	4	G	7-	0-	6-	5
D7 (9)	6-	8-	5-	0	G	10-	0-	8-	7
D7	6-	2-	3-	0	G	10-	7-	8-	0
D7	4-	0-	5-	6	G	10-	7-	8-	10
D7	4-	6-	5-	0	G	10-	12-	10-	10
D7	6-	2-	3-	4	G	0-	0-	1-	3
D maj7 (9)	6½-	0-	7-	8	G maj7	2-	0-	1-	3
D maj7 or min7	6½-	0-	7-	9	G maj7	5-	0-	5-	3
D7	9-	6-	0-	7	G maj7	3-	0-	5-	5
D maj7	9-6½-	7-		0	G maj7	9-	0-	8-	10
D7	9-	6-	7-	0	G9	3-	0-	0-	5
					G sus4	6-	0-	6-	6

D-D-A-D

Chords	T	T	M	B	Chords	T	T	M	B
A	4-	1-	2-	1	B sus⁴	2-	1-	1-	2
A or Am	1-	0-	1-	1	B sus⁴	8-	5-	5-	5
A	6½-	4-	4-	4	Bm⁹ ⁽¹¹⁾	8-	5-	6-	0
A	1-	1-	2-	4					
A¹¹	6½-	4-	0-	4	Em	1-	1-	1-	1
Am	6-	4-	4-	4	Em	1-	3-	1-	1
Am¹¹	6-	0-	4-	4	Em	3-	1-	1-	1
Am¹¹	6-	8-	7-	0	Em	3-	3-	1-	1
Am¹¹	6-	8-	0-	0	Em	5-	3-	4-	5
Am	8-	6-	0-	6	E or Em	8-	8-	8-	8
A⁷ ⁽¹¹⁾	3-	0-	0-	6	Em⁷	3-	0-	1-	1
A or Am	4-	4-	4-	4	Em⁷	1-	0-	1-	3
A or Am	4-	1-	0-	1	Em⁷	1-	3-	1-	0
A¹¹	4-6½-		4-	0	Em⁷	3-	0-	4-	5
A¹¹	1-	0-	2-	4	Em⁷	7-	3-	4-	5
Am¹¹	4-	0-	4-	6	Em⁷	8-	10-	8-	0
Am⁷	6-	3-	4-	4	Em⁷⁽¹³⁾	8-	10-	9-	0
A sus⁴	4-	0-	4-	4	Em⁶	8-	5-	6-	6
A sus⁴	4-	0-	0-	1	Em¹¹	8-	3-	4-	5
A sus⁴	7-	0-	4-	4	Em⁷	5-	3-	4-	0
A sus⁴	7-	4-	4-	4	E	5-	5-6½-		8
A⁷	4-	3-	2-	1	E⁷	5-	0-6½-		8
A sus⁴	7-	0-	7-	8	E⁷ aug	6-	0-6½-		8
A⁷	10-6½-		7-	8	Em⁷	7-	10-	8-	0
Bm	2-	0-	1-	2	C	6-	6-	4-	3
Bm	5-	7-	5-	5	C⁹	3-	6-	4-	0
Bm	5-	7-	5-	0	C⁹	3-	0-	4-	6
Bm	5-	2-	3-	0	C⁹	6-	8-	6-	0
Bm	5-	0-	5-	5	C⁹	6-	0-	4-	3
Bm	0-	0-	1-	2	Cmaj⁷	6-	3-	4-	5
Bm	7-	0-	5-	5					
Bm	9-	7-	8-	0	F#m	2-	2-	2-	4
Bm	2-	0-	3-	5	F# or F#m	2-	2-	2-	2
Bm¹¹	2-	0-	1-	1	F# or F#m	9-	9-	9-	9
Bm¹¹	8-	5-	5-	7	F#m⁷⁽¹¹⁾	8-	5-	6-	5
Bm⁷ ⁽¹¹⁾	4-	0-	4-	5	F#m	4-	4-	2-	2
Bm⁷	4-	0-	1-	2					
Bm⁹	5-	7-	6-	0	C#m	1-	1-	2-	1

D-D-G-D

Chords	T	T	M	B	Chords	T	T	M	B
G or Gm	0-	0-	0-	3	C⁹	6-	0-	7-	8
G	3-	0-	2-	3	C⁹	6-	8-	7-	0
G	3-	0-	4-	5	C⁶⁽⁹⁾	6-	3-	4-	4
G	5-	3-	0-	3	C⁶⁽⁹⁾	3-	0-	3-	4
G	5-	3-	4-	5	C⁹	6-	0-	5-	0
G	5-	0-	0-	7					
G	5-	0-	0-	5	C# dim	8-6½-		7-	8
G	3-	5-	4-	3					
G	3-	5-	4-	0	D	2-	0-	1-	2
G or Gm	10-	7-	0-	7	D	2-	0-	1-	0
G or Gm	10-	0-	0-	10	D	2-	0-	4-	0
G	10-	12-	11-	0	D	2-	0-	4-	4
G	10-	0-	0-	12	D or Dm	4-	0-	4-	4
G	10-	0-	9-	10	D	4-	0-	4-	0
G	7-	10-	0-	7	D	4-	2-	4-	0
G	7-	0-	0-	7	D	9-	0-	8-	0
G	7-	0-	7-	0	D	9-	0-	8-	9
G	3-	0-	0-	3	D	9-	7-	8-	0
G	3-	0-	0-	5	D	7-	4-6½-		0
G sus⁴	3-	0-	3-	0	D	7-	0-6½-		0
G sus⁴	3-	0-	4-	6	D	7-	0-	8-	9
G sus⁴	6-	0-	0-	6	D	7-	0-6½-		4
G sus⁴	6-	7-	7-	0	D⁷	2-	0-	3-	4
G⁷	5-	0-	6-	0	D⁷	4-	0-	3-	4
G⁶⁽⁹⁾	4-	1-	2-	3	D⁷	4-	6-6½-		0
G⁹	4-	0-	5-	7	D⁷	6-	7-6½-		0
Gmaj⁷	7-	0-	0-	9	D⁷	9-	11-	10-	0
					D⁷	0-	6-6½-		0
C	1-	3-	3-	3	D⁷	6-	0-6½-		7
C⁹	6-	0-	0-	8	D⁷	2-	4-	3-	0
C⁹	1-	0-	3-	3	D⁷	4-	0-	4-	6
C⁹	3-	0-	5-	6	D⁷	4-	6-	4-	0
C⁹	3-	0-	3-	1	Dmaj⁷	6½-	9-	8-	0

D-D-G-D

Chords	T	T	M	B		Chords	T	T	M	B
D sus⁴	7-	4-	0-	4		E or Em	1-	1-	2-	1
D sus⁴	7-	0-	8-	10		Em	1-	3-	2-	3
D sus⁴	2-	0-	0-	4		Em	3-	1-	2-	3
D sus⁴	9-	0-	0-	11		Em⁷	1-	0-	0-	1
D sus⁴	4-	0-	0-	4		Em⁷	1-	0-	0-	3
Dm	4-	0-	6-	4		Em⁷	1-	0-	2-	3
Dm⁷	7-	6-	6-	0		Em⁷	1-	3-	2-	0
Dm⁷	6-	0-	6-	6		Em⁷	5-	0-	7-	8
Dm⁷	6-	7-	6-	0		Em⁷	10-	8-	0-	7
Dm⁷	7-	4-	6-	0		Em⁷	8-	10-	9-	0
Dm⁷	4-	0-	6-	6		Em⁷	8-	0-	0-	10
Dm⁷	7-	6-	6-	0		E or Em⁷	5-	8-	7-	0
Dm⁹	6-	0-	6-	8		Em⁷	7-	0-	7-	8
Dm⁹	6-	8-	6-	0		E or Em⁷	5-	0-	5-	5
Dm⁹	4-	0-	5-	0		Em⁷	8-	0-	7-	8
Dmaj⁷⁽⁹⁾	6½-	8-6½-	0			Em⁶	8-6½-	7-	7	
D⁹	1-	0-	1-	2		Em¹¹	1-	4-	2-	3
						F	6-	4-	6-	4
Am	6-	4-	5-	6		F or Fm	6-	6-	6-	6
A	6½-	4-	5-6½							
A	6½-	4-	5-	4		F♯m⁷	2-	1-	1-	2
A or Am	1-	1-	1-	1						
A⁹	4-	1-	2-	4		Bm	9-	0-	9-	9
A sus⁴	1-	0-	1-	1		Bm	9-	12-	11-	0
A sus⁴	1-	0-	1-	4		Bm	5-	7-6½-	0	
A sus⁴	7-	4-	5-	4		Bm	2-	0-	4-	5
A sus⁴	8-	0-	8-	8		Bm	5-	0-	4-	5
A sus⁴	4-	0-	5-6½			Bm	2-	0-	2-	2
A⁹	6½-	4-	5-	5		Bm	5-	0-	2-	2
A⁷ sus⁴	1-	0-	1-	3		Bm⁷	2-	4-	2-	0
Am¹¹	1-	0-	3-	4		Bm⁷	5-	0-	2-	2
Am⁷⁽¹¹⁾	4-	0-	0-	6		Bm¹¹	5-	8-6½-	0	
Am¹¹	4-	0-	5-	6		Bm¹¹	2-	0-	2-	1
Am⁷	6-	3-	3-	4		Bm¹¹	1-	0-	2-	2
Am¹¹	4-	0-	5-	6		B dim	5-	0-	6-	7
Am¹¹	7-	4-	5-	6		B dim	5-	7-	6-	0
Am¹¹	8-	11-	10-	0						

PLAYING DULCIMER IN JAM SESSIONS
By Holly Tannen

Fiddlers and banjo players have been known to roll their eyes and gaze into space when a dulcimer player pulls up a chair. Sometimes, after doggedly playing along and gaining their acceptance, I ask them the reason for this prejudice against dulcimers. They tell me that they worry that the dulcimer will only be able to play in the key to which it is tuned, that the drones will be discordant with the chord shifts of banjo and guitar, and that the bom-biddy-bomp strumming may obscure melodic subtleties. Through years of messing around, I've developed some easy solutions to these problems, so that the dulcimer can blend in with string music of many styles.

Most fiddle tunes have the shape AABB: you play an eight-bar phrase, repeat it, then play another eight-bar phrase and repeat that. To play along, you need to learn, by trial and error, the chord changes of each phrase.

I play a three-stringed dulcimer tuned D, D, and D an octave below, for a bright, mandolin-like sound. I use .010 or .012 for the melody and middle strings, and a bronze-wound .026 for the bass. Looking at the fretboard chart, you can see that if you fret all three strings at the first fret you will fret three E notes; at the second fret, three F♯s, and so on. I fret the melody string with my ring finger, the middle string with my middle finger, and the bass string with my index finer. This leaves my left thumb free to improvise above the chord.

Placing the thumb two frets above the chord will create a "third" that is sometimes minor, sometimes major, which means that sometimes it will fit in with your tune and sometimes it won't. When playing the A chord, at the fourth fret, put your thumb on the 6½ fret, three frets above to play A major; on the sixth fret to play A minor. This chord, three fingers down on any fret, sometimes with, sometimes without, the thumb two frets above it, can move all over the fretboard to create a clear and simple chord back-up.

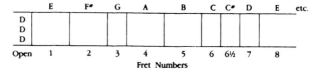

The most pervasive chord in any tune is called the I chord or tonic. Tunes almost invariably end on the tonic. The chord to which tunes most frequently shift is the V chord or dominant. When I hear the chord shift from the tonic, I try the V chord first. If the V sounds wrong, I try the IV chord or subdominant.

Key	Tonic I	Subdominant IV	Dominant V	Relative Minor VIm
D	D 07 / 07 / 07	G 33 / 33 / 35	A 44 / 44 / 46½	Bm 55 / 55 / 57
G	G 33 / 33 / 35	C 66 / 66 / 68	D 07 / 07 / 07	Em 1 / 1 / 3
A	A 44 / 44 / 46½	D 07 / 07 / 07	E 18 / 18 / 18	$F\#m$ 22 / 22 / 24

Dulcimer tuning:	D / D / D	Am = 4 / 4 / 6	C#m = 6½ / 6½ / 6½

Looking at the fretboard chart, play the chord progression I, IV, V, and back to I, in the key of D. Then play the same progression in the key of G, and in the key of A. Then play through them all again, adding your thumb two frets above each chord: it should sound "good" everywhere except on the A chord (put your thumb instead on the 6½ fret, three frets above the chord), and the E becomes an Em chord when thumb is placed two frets above.

Many American fiddle tunes use only these three chords; each tune has its own pattern of chord changes. A few tunes use the relative minor, which is found two frets below the tonic: in D, Bm (5th fret chord); in G, Em (first fret chord); and in A, F# minor (second fret chord). In each case you can add your thumb two frets above for a minor sound.

Irish tunes may have other shapes, some simpler, some more complex, than American tunes. Many do nothing more than rock back and forth between a minor chord and the major chord on the fret below it (the VII chord), with perhaps a V chord right before the last tonic chord of a phrase. the first phrase of "Sligo Maid," for example, goes Am, G, Am, G, E, Am. Similarly, a tune may move between Dm and C (for instance, "Banish Misfortune"), between Bm and A ("The Musical Priest"), or between Em and D ("The Butterfly"). A tune may occasionally go to the major chord two frets above the tonic: in Em, G major; in Bm, D major, in Am, C major.

I learned to follow these patterns by trial and error. I play quietly at the edge of a session if I'm not familiar with the tunes and expect to flounder a lot. I may ask the guitarist to call out the chord changes. I choose groups who play each tune many times over, rather than the hot Irish players who string many tunes together, playing each one only twice through. I've learned not to harass myself when I make a "mistake" but to see it as part of the process. It is less important to get the chord shifts exactly right than it is to play solid rhythm. I may close my eyes in order to really hear the fiddler's lines. If there are only a couple of instruments, I may try to underline the fiddle's rhythm exactly. If there are many instruments, I'll strum less, perhaps just accenting the first and third beat of each four-beat bar.

So: run through these chord progressions, look for compatible people to play with, and don't let fear of making "mistakes" freeze your fingers up. It's all process, and you have a lifetime of music ahead of you.

APPENDICES

Notes that occur in the five diatonic modes which appear in on the charts. Please note that the 6½ fret is included. Ignore that value if your dulcimer does not have the fret.

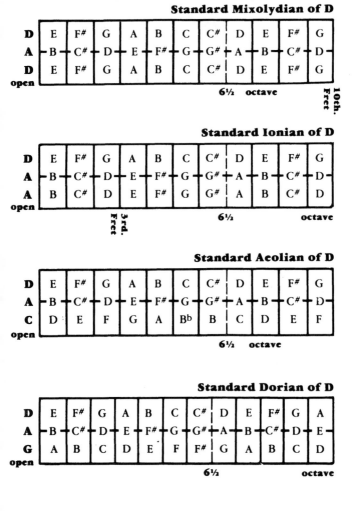

C	D	E	F	G	A	Bb	B	C	D	E	F	G	A	Bb
G	A	B	C	D	E	F	F#	G	A	B	C	D	E	F
D	E	F#	G	A	B	C	C#	D	E	F#	G	A	B	C

Open   6½   octave

MODES: A BRIEF HISTORY

Hermes, the son of Zeus, is the mythological forerunner of the modes. After stealing some of Apollo's prize cattle, he fashioned a lyre utilizing the intestines of the cattle for strings. Upon being caught by Apollo, Hermes redeemed himself by singing praises to him on his four-string harp. Apollo was so impressed with the music flowing from the harp that he took it in exchange for the cattle.

The four-string lyre is one of the earliest instruments of Greek civilization. Based upon this lyre, the tetrachord, one of the earliest scales in western music, was developed. The tetrachord was a series of four notes within an interval of a fourth. It consisted of a whole tone, whole tone, ½ tone.

Tetrachord of E:

E, D, C, B.

Te, Tw, Tn, Ta: Greek names for the tetrachord.

The Greek scales were in descending order, not ascending order as our present western scales. The keys, or relative pitch, to the Greeks was much different from what we use in music today. In a tetrachord the first and last notes are always in a fourth of each other. As with much of Greek philosophy and science, the most important interval in music was the perfect fourth. By placing two tetrachords together the scale was formulated.

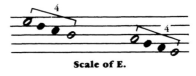

Scale of E.

The oldest scale or mode was the Dorian, which had the same notes as the original tetrachord: E, D, C, B, A, G, F, E.

The term diatonic refers to the lowest and highest tones in the tetrachord always being a fourth apart. The distance between the second and third notes were movable and the ½ step could be anywhere between the first and the fourth tone. Thus, the diatonic tetrachord consisted of two whole tones and one ½ tone.

$$\overbrace{E}^{1} \quad \overbrace{D}^{1} \quad \overbrace{C}^{½} \quad B$$

The Greeks used the Phrygian, Lydian, Aeolian and Iastian modes, as well as the Dorian. For each of these, there were three modes. That is, the principal, say the Dorian, then a mode which started a fourth below (Hypo-Dorian) and one a fourth above (Hyper-Dorian).

Fourth below	Principal	Fourth above
Hypo-Dorian B, A, G, F	Dorian E, D, C, B	Hyper-Dorian A, G, F, E
Hypo-Phrygian A, G, F, E	Phrygian D, C, B, A	Hyper-Phrygian G, F, E, D
Hypo-Lydian G, F, E, D	Lydian C, B, A, G	Hyper-Lydian F, E, D, C
Hypo-Aeolian F, E, D, C	Aeolian B, A, G, F	Hyper-Aeolian E, D, C, B
Hypo-Iastian E, D, C, B	Iastian A, G, F, E	Hyper-Iastian D, C, B, A

Each tetrachord was a mode. Thus, there were 15 modes until the time of Ptolemy (130 A.D.). Once again the tetrachords are in descending order and the relative pitch is not the same as A = 440 cps.

Thus, in the beginning all the original modes were formed from the Greek lyre tuned to the perfect fourth of E, D, C, B. The Dorian was the oldest and most admired mode and sired "The Complete System", which was a series of tones spanning two octaves and composed of four Dorian tetrachords. Each arrangement of tones and semitones gave birth to a new mode. Therefore, the diatonic system was a formation of tones (2) and semitones (1) within a tetrachord.

The legendary figure who scientifically fixed the modes was Pythagoras (584-504 B.C.). Born in Samos, he was educated in Egypt for 22 years, where he became an initiate in the arts of mathematics, philosophy, astronomy and astrology. The Egyptians had the same myths and theories surrounding the birth of music and the modes as the Greeks. During this period of time the Greeks and Egyptians traded freely. It has even been theorized that the Greeks learned this knowledge from the Egyptians as did the Chaldeans, Phonecians, Ethioptians and Hebrews. In each of these cultures the number 4 (from the tetrachord) and the number 7 (notes in a scale) were sacred. After returning from Egypt, Pythagoras went to Babylonia and then spent the remainder of his life in Italy.

Pythagoras unified the octave with the scale and established the perfect 5th. Legend has it that he added the 8th. note to the seven-string harp of Terpander and added the 5th. (B note) to the Dorian scale. Therefore, Pythagoras was the perfecter of the scale by uniting the two tetrachords of Terpander.

He used a one-stringed instrument (monochord) with movable bridges to fix the ratio of the octave (1:2), the 5th. (2:3) and the 4th. (3:4). Pythagoras and his followers believed numbers were within everything and represented all of creation. Using the monochord, he theorized that the seven known planets, revolving in perfect circles on invisible spheres, were in the same proportion to each other as the notes on the scale. The harmony emitted by the interval and spacing of these planets produced a concordant sound, the music of the spheres. It was a belief at this time that the oldest modes, Dorian, Phrygian and Lydian, were ruled by various planets. Thus, the modes took on certain astrological characteristics. The music emitted by the planetary spheres was believed to have a great influence on mortal beings. Here are some comments on the ancient modes.

The Dorian: Ruled by Saturn, bestower of wisdom, quality of response, and dignity. Folk tunes: "John Barleycorn", "Greensleeves", "Darkness, Darkness".

The Phrygian: Ruled by Mars, fury and warlike, used to march Spartans into battle. Playing an oboe in this mode was a cure for sciatica. To Aristotle it was a power of inspiration. Compositions: Beethoven's "String Quartet in Am", Ralph Williams' "Fantasia" on a theme of Thomas Tallis, "The White Paternoster", "Pretty Polly".

The Lydian: Ruled by Jupiter, sharpens one's wit. Aristotle said it had the power of healing and awakening, love of purity and modesty. Plato said it had a sensuous nature, best suited for orgies. Pythagoras is said to have soothed a youth who was in an erotic rage by playing in the Lydian Mode. "Ever against eating cares, lap me in soft lydian airs" . . . John Milton (L'Allegro). Folk tunes: "The Woods So Wild", "Miles" by Richard Farina.

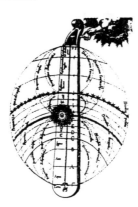

Latter Modes:

The Mixolydian: Ruled by the sun. Not utilized very much until the Gregorian Chants. Fiddle tunes: "Little Beggerman", "Bonapart's Retreat".

The Ionian: Playful and happy. Due to this it was excluded by the Church. Tunes: "Old Mother Flannagan", "Jolly Rogues of Lynn".

The Aeolian: Appeases the mind. Tunes: "Nunsuch", "Shady Grove", "Scarborough Faire"

The Locrian: Due to its scale it has not been used very much. However, in a piece on the modes by Roger Nichelson I found a contemporary tune exists in the Locrian by John Kirkpatrick called "Ashes to Ashes"

By playing in the right mode at the right time Pythagoras is said to have defeated 5,000 Sybrite Calvarymen with the power of a flute. Shortly after his death, his student Pindar wrote the famous Pythian Mode to honor him. The Pythian Mode does not exceed an interval of four tones a la the tetrachord. The use of modes in the Pythagorean tradition was kept alive by his followers, like Pindar, Pisistratues and Timotheus.

In 350 B.C. a pupil of Aristotle named Aristoxenus opposed the Pythagorean method of mathematical calculation. He arranged the mode intervals by ear and his school became known as the harmonists and opposed the latter Pythagoreans who were called canonists. Aristoxenus based everything on the senses for musical purposes and rejected the idea of vibration, proportions and velocities. For example, the ½ tone to Aristoxenus was shown to be in the proportion of 256:243.

Euclid (277 B.C.) utilized the monochord to demonstrate the science of harmonics, sounds, intervals, keys and melopia. He scientifically set the octave as somewhat less than six whole tones. Euclid was the first to actually write out the proportions propagated by Pythagoras.

Didymus (63 B.C.-10 A.D.), an honoured musician of the emperor Nero, made a great contribution to modal history. He was the first to introduce the major and minor third to the diatonic scale, which helped to harmonize the entire system.

Ptolemy (130 A.D.) was the reformer of the modes by making the octave the regulator of the scale. Until this time the modes were still divided into tetrachords. The 4th. was the most important aspect of the Greek scale and so there were 15 modes. By using the octave instead of the 4th., Ptolemy reduced the modes to the seven we know today. He ordered the pitch of the modes and set them a semi-tone above each other.

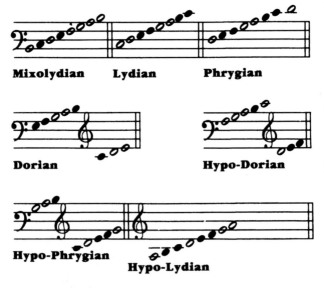

*Burnay: *A General History of Music*, pg. 56.

Like Pythagoras, Ptolemy believed the modes were influenced by the motions of the planets. It should be remembered that to many of these ancient Greek thinkers astronomy, astrology, mathematics and music were all interrelated.

The Church Modes

St. Ambrose (340-397), the Bishop of Milan, was the first to employ the original Greek modes (Dorian, Phrygian, Lydian and Mixolydian) for the Church, known as Ambrosian chants. Ambrose developed a method for chanting the Psalms, which was spread throughout North Africa by St. Augustine.

Mode

I Dorian: D E F G a b c d
II Phrygian: E F G A b c d e
III Lydian: F G A B c d e f
IV Mixolydian: G A B C d e f g

The Church modes were similar to the Greek in name only. The pattern of the intervals made it impossible to modulate key and the range of these modes was limited to mostly one octave.

The famous composer Mendelssohn once commented on this limiting factor of the Church modes by stating, "I can't help it, but it does irritate me to hear such holy and touching words sung to such dull, drawling music."

Pope Gregory (450-604) increased the ecclesiastical modes to eight by adding four plagel modes which started a 4th. below the authentic modes utilized by Ambrose. Once again these were done simply and were similar to the original Greek modes in name only.

Mode

Dorian	D E F G A B C D
Hypo-Dorian	A B C D E F G A
Phrygian	E F G A B C D
Hypo-Phrygian	B C DE F G A B
Lydian	F G A B C D E F
Hypo-Lydian	C D EF G A B C
Mixolydian	G A B C D E F G
Hypo-Mixolydian	D E F G A B C D

In 1547 a Swiss monk, Henry of Glareanes, added the Aeolian (A) and its plagel (E) and the Ionian (C) and its plagel (G).

The original Greek modes have survived in the form of traditional folk music. One need only look at the Cecil Sharp collections or O'Neill's book of Irish Music to see the large proportion of tunes and ballads still played in modes. The tribe who settled the British Isles in 3 A.D. (the Kelts) lived in northern and eastern Europe and a few of the Keltic tribes migrated into Greece in 350 B.C. Speculative as it may seem, one might venture a guess that the Kelts may have learned this modal system of music at the same time as the Greeks, Egyptians, Chaldeans, Phönecians and Hebrews. A great deal of the music that came to America from the British Isles is of a modal nature. Folk melodies that we play today might have their roots 2,000 years or more in the past.

Bibliography

Barton, Todd, "Analogia: Musica Mundana and Musica Humana", *Pro Musica Magazine*, January-February 1976, pp. 7-9.

Burney, Charles, *A General History of Music*, Dover, 1957. A reprint from the first edition: 1776. Re-edited by Frak Mercer.

Murchie, Guy, *Music of the Spheres*, Vol. 2, Dover Publications, 1961.

Naumann, Emil, *The History of Music*, Vol. I, Cassell & Company Ltd.

Nicholson, Roger, *Modal Music*. From *The Dulcimer Songbook*, Oak Publications, 1978.

Pratt, Waldo Selden, *The History of Music*, G. Schirmer, 1907.

Smoldon, William L., *A History of Music*, Dimension Books, 1966.

GOURD MUSIC
P r e s e n t s

Recordings by Neal Hellman

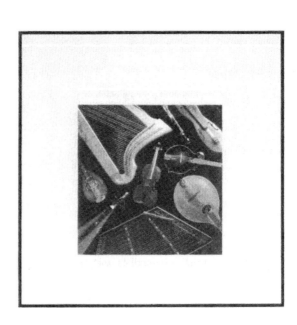

GOURD MUSIC
Post Office Box 585
Felton, California 95018